The Caregiver Companion

The Caregiver Companion

Love's Burden and Holding On Through His Mercy

Redemptions Rhythms: Interpretive Companion Book 5

D. BRANDT

RESOURCE *Publications* • Eugene, Oregon

THE CAREGIVER COMPANION
Love's Burden and Holding On Through His Mercy

Redemptions Rhythms: Interpretive Companion, Book 5

Resource Publications
An Imprint of Wipf and Stock Publishers
199 W. 8th Ave., Suite 3
Eugene, OR 97401

www.wipfandstock.com

PAPERBACK ISBN: 979-8-3852-9209-7
HARDCOVER ISBN: 979-8-3852-9210-3
EBOOK ISBN: 979-8-3852-9211-0

VERSION NUMBER 07/31/26

Redemptions Rhythms: Interpretive Companion

Held
In *Redemptions*
Through *Deliverance*
By *Redemptions Refrain*

To Providence, Spouses, and Caregivers who—
Love completely
Give freely
Hold nothing back

Contents

Part III—Mercy in the Unraveling

Note to the Reader

Caregiving is not a single moment, but a way of living. What begins as small acts—helping with a task, repeating a conversation, offering support—becomes a steady pattern of care. These acts accumulate, and over time, they reshape daily life.

This work is written for spouses, children, family members, pastors, and friends who care for others. It is also written for those who seek to understand that work from the outside.

Caregiving places strain not only on the body, but on communication, understanding, and expectation. Words are repeated, forgotten, or misunderstood. Needs return again and again. Meaning is often carried not through explanation, but through presence.

The poems in this volume reflect that experience. Repetition, refrain, and variation are not simply formal choices—they arise from the daily rhythms of caregiving itself, where tasks return, emotions cycle, and resolution is often delayed or absent.

Some of the poems in this book are returning poems from earlier books in this series. Returning poems are noted beneath the poem using book titles or abbreviated identifiers.

The Interpretive Companion appears on the facing pages. It is not a summary. It is an intentional equivalent, offering another way of entering what the Message expresses. The Message and its Companion stand side by side, with the reader engaging both.

These poems are meant to be read slowly, allowing the interplay between Message and Companion to reflect the lived experience of caregiving—where understanding is not always immediate, but is often formed through patience, attention, and love.

Series Note

THIS VOLUME IS BOOK 5 in the series *Redemptions Rhythms: Interpretive Companion*. The series pairs the Message—often formal, high-structure poetry—with its Interpretive Companion to guide readers through lived experiences where language, understanding, and control begin to falter.

This fifth volume focuses on love's burden and holding on through His mercy, presenting these themes through a structured Message and its Interpretive Companion.

Brandt Triadic Villanelle designates a triadic villanelle form developed by D. Brandt and used throughout this series.

Unending devotion balms journey's tomb,
When the day to day breaks the loom—
stubborn joy keeps you in the ring.

Teaches the how to make days sing—
Makes each moment in the now.
Time to grace, it does not bow—
Grace gives back the time ill spent.
It does not deign life's day repent—
But rather that it is let live.

Our daily forms move on and give—
They promenade devoted, nigh.
With God not brash, or scarce or staged—
but faithful, silent, and engaged.

Caregiver's Couplets

Unending devotion balms journey's tomb.
Daily struggles wear you down—
stubborn joy keeps you in the ring.

Life stays vibrant this is how—
Make each moment in the now.
Grace does not stop time—
it redeems the moment.
Grace does not interrupt life—
it reveals it.

The pattern does not end—
it walks with us.
Providence is not rare, loud, or theatrical—
but faithful, quiet, and near.

Cheryl walks in faithful strength,
Love's joy sustained through marriage length.
Mother's life did guide my way—
Her memories transform today.
Silent caregivers abide
Loved one's burdens that do hide.
And God, whose mercies hold
Loving charges redemptive fold.

Acknowledgments

For Cheryl, whose quiet faithfulness, strength, and love have sustained me through every burden shared and every joy remembered.

For my mother, whose life and memory continue to shape my own.

For caregivers, spouses, children, pastors, and friends who quietly bear burdens for others, often unseen.

And above all, for Providence, whose mercy does not interrupt life, but reveals it.

Caregiving incremental grows—
Little steps rage into a flow.

For spouse and child and pastor's love—
Formal verse births meaning above.

Love's mercy shown when bodies fall—
By holding fast to mercy's shawl.

Refrain repeats in endless grind—
Villanelles loop care's failing mind.

Companion leads does not replace—
Guides the reader to find their place.

This book moves through caregiver's life—
The work they do, failed functions rife.

What's tiring, holy, unresolved—
Providence holds what's not absolved.

Introduction

Caregiving unfolds through repetition. What is done once is done again, and then again—meals prepared, questions answered, routines followed, and needs met that do not resolve but return. Over time, this repetition becomes the structure of daily life.

What begins as occasional help becomes sustained responsibility. The body grows tired. The mind grows weary. The work continues.

In this work, love is not shown through dramatic moments, but through persistence. It appears in steady presence, in small acts, in patience that must be renewed daily. What is given is not always recognized. What is done does not always change the outcome.

The structure of this volume reflects that experience. Cyclical forms, repeated lines, and patterned rhythms mirror the lived reality of caregiving, where days echo one another and progress is not always visible.

The Interpretive Companion stands alongside each poem as a parallel expression. Where the Message may compress experience into formal structure, the Companion offers another voice—not to replace it, but to accompany it. Together, they create a space in which the reader can approach the same reality from more than one direction.

This volume moves through the life of caregiving: the early sharing of burdens, the sustained work of holding on, and the later seasons where strength, memory, and clarity begin to fail. It does not resolve these experiences. It remains within them.

Caregiving is shown here as it is lived—tiring, repetitive, often unseen, and deeply human. Yet within that work, love endures, and what is held is not without meaning.

PART I

Love's Burden Shared

Caregiving often begins quietly. Love takes on new burdens little by little: helping with chores, repeating conversations, managing appointments, or simply remaining present. These poems explore the first shared weight of caregiving, where love begins to carry more than it once did.

Reading with the Companion

The Companion offers a parallel expression, drawing out meaning where language strains or fails. Read the Message on the right and its Companion on the left together or move between them as needed.

I.1

I must opine apology.
Husband and I are not here
Domestic chores and this and that,
Made our abode far more neat.

These tasks now done I'll talk to you,
Though shopping soon will not do.
Hubby and I are snuggling now,
We will see you all real soon.

I.1
Michelle's Split Focus

Sorry, sorry! I wasn't done.
Hubby and I are on the run
Rearranging the furniture,
Patio's better to be sure.

OK, I'm done, what do you want,
Grocery shopping? Hate to hunt.
We'll just stay here and sit around,
Let everyone else go to town.

Redemptions VI.2

I.2

Is everyone stupid?
It seems that way;
Or mentally deficient,
Is that more correct?

But my reflection
Makes me see,
That all of me,
And you too—are no better!

Yet we need not obsess,
Or speak in anger;
Jesus fully gives love,
Strengthens our hearts with grace.

I.2
Mirror's Redemption

Is all the world a moron?
Sometimes it seems to be;
Or is it rather retard,
Is what some might see?

But when I look in mirrors
I soon do realize,
That me, myself, and I,
And you—are flawed likewise!

Yet this need not consume us,
Prompt bitter, angry words;
For Jesus gives love fully,
His love's grace the heart girds.

Deliverance II.6

I.3

Youth imagines tomorrow forever,
Treats strength as always,
Assumes life's road stretches to end of time.
Time quietly refuses such brashness.

Bodies weaken despite protest,
Dreams narrow, nightmares emerge,
Opportunities pass unreturned,
And pride learns it is not enough.

Yet aging is not merely loss.
Later years strip illusion away,
Teaching that ordinary moments are limited,
And Providence holds us when vigor flees.

I.3
Aging's Clarity

Sober later years

Time is unyielding to man

Once blind now I see

I.4

Faraway eyes useless and hidden:
Once present but no longer.
He, I, and all seem trapped in emptiness:
Where is the goodness in God's thoughts?
Quiet sorrow deafens all:
Muffled in solitude.
Calling out to his mother, unheard:
But Providence's love forever remains.

I.4
Son Taken

Distant eyes unseeing, unseen:
He who was here is not.
Emptiness with me, him, and tween:
What good hath God's mind wrought?
Silent grief unhearing, unheard:
Isolation muted.
Reached out to his mom but no word:
Yet God's endless love is rooted.

PART II

The Work of Holding On

Once caregiving becomes part of daily life, the work shifts from noticing decline to enduring it. Fear, exhaustion, physical weakness, and the strain of loving well all come to the surface. These poems explore the difficult work of holding on when strength, certainty, and control begin to fail.

II.1

Derriere bound—traveling by air—
Squashed by my sacroiliac.
Oh to be young again,
This life trial wasn't planned.

Tomorrow is Providence's job,
It's above my pay grade.
Momma says, "Old age sucks big time"—
It reveals we are weaklings—
And makes us look elsewhere for fortitude
Like to him who went farther than anyone else
To save humanity from the mess we are in
And give fortitude so you don't disappear
Into the void of desperation,
Tied up and clueless in the blackest of nights.

So, by this might beyond my own
I set myself apart to you.
I put myself into certain care,
Beseeching Him for safe landing.

II.1
Sure Hands

Sitting here—I'm waiting for plane—
Contemplating lower back pain.
Never had this as a young man,
Vicissitudes not in my plan.

But future stuff is in God's realm,
Not meant that I should take that helm.
To quote my momma, "Old age sucks"—
And shows you that you aren't that tough—
And forces you to seek your strength
Within the one who went great lengths
To rescue man from life's great stink
And give you strength so you don't sink
Into obscurity, despair,
Bound in a dark place unawares.

So, by this power not from me
I consecrate myself to Thee
I place myself into sure hands,
Praying to Him that my plane lands.

Deliverance IV.2

II.2

Entwined by Adam's possessed curse
Daily dread does rise and thrive
Concerning running's berth
Pace ever easing to the worse
Sanity guides thinking's guise
Pace still easing to the worse
Thick gooey syrup in verse
Cannot easily affranchise
Life waxes full, with joy disperse
When this mindset one does immerse
To ever fill each moments rise
In full possess existence terse

II.2
Defying Age

As I grow old
Fears do grow
That my running
Will grow slow
And my thinking
Grow slow too
Cold molasses
Just won't do
Life stays vibrant
This is how
Make each moment
In the now

Redemptions VI.4

II.3

Worn out spirit, soul, and body;
I'm distressed by the toil of doing good.
Not my desires—it's beyond me—
God must intervene.

By your touch soothe my deep hurts;
Bandage body's tangle to comfort and quiet.
Yet sweet Father I'm governed by anxiety—
I'm burdened by death's garment.

Traveling in torment
Where hopelessness is woven into me;
Ache strips and cuts it out,
Then I feel the depth of pain.

I can't do what is required,
Being tied up and bound;
Untangle my soul's bondage—my course dies—
Transform and immerse me wholly in your love.

II.3
Love Baptize

Tired body, tired mind;
I am stressed by kindness grind.
What I want is not the need—
Providence must intercede.

In your hands my deep pains balm,
Bind life's knot to soothe and calm;
But dear Abba fear does reign—
Body's weighted linen strain.

Down the path of agony
Looms despair's life tapestry;
Pain removed when threads excised,
Poet's hurt then realized.

And my skills don't match this need,
Nimble fingers not yet freed;
Unthread my flesh—my way dies—
Dye my soul, with love baptize.

Deliverance IV.5 and *Relationship* III.1

II.4

Jesus loves me this I know.
More than the Bible tells me so:
Redemption bought by His death in love,
Now He lives love—everything has changed.
His mercy and love redeemed me
And gave me a life to love.
Today the good news struggle starts:
Love and mercy despite humanity's noise.

II.4
Mercy's Love

The love of Jesus this I know,
Not just the Bible tells me so:
Deliverance by death's love came,
His life's love now—never the same.
For He by mercy's love did save
With love's new life to me He gave.
Now gospel's struggle does begin:
Mercy's love in Adam's din.

Deliverance IV.3 and Redemptions Refrain V.3

II.5

Possession is grabbing me—
Poetry fixation births inspired verse.
Anxiety quells over poor rhyme,
Uneven rhythm, uninspired poem.

Night terrors lose their fright
The mind's control forsakes gloom;
Alarm is quieted, joy is here
Hope has replaced my dark spirit.

II.5
Fear Erased

My obsession taking hold—
Poem's focus, verse's gold.
Fears abate of lacking rhyme,
Stumbling rhythm, missing chime.

Deep night's day is lacking fear
For mind's sway abandons drear;
Dread is gone, delight has come
Hope has swapped with spirit's glum.

Redemptions Refrain IV.4

PART III

Mercy in the Unraveling

Caregiving eventually enters places where body and mind begin to fail. In those moments, caregiving becomes less about fixing and more about remaining. These poems explore how love survives when intellect, strength, and certainty do not.

III.1

Quiet unraveling intellect shrivels mental core,
Swallowing the day's song with drudgery
As Benevolence soothes grisly chaotic beast,
Quietly concealing bitter confusion's end,
With harsh growths overtaking one's being.
Quiet unraveling intellect shrivels mental core,
Masks awareness by destruction's bleakest cover
By way of lost recollection formerly adored—
Foretells sorrow's shift, frustrating thought's path,
Condemning lost intellect now irrelevant
As life's knowledge ceases.
Quiet unraveling intellect shrivels mental core,
Lifelong remembrance never again clear.
Kindness answers what intellect no longer speaks,
As Benevolence soothes grisly chaotic beast.
Quiet unraveling intellect shrivels mental core,
Foretells sorrow's shift, frustrating thought's path,
Removes deep sorrow with love's understanding—
As Benevolence soothes grisly chaotic beast.

III.1
Providence's Balm

Silent mental tangles wither mind's root,
Subsuming daily lived rhythm with grind
While Providence balms dark confusion's brute,
Slyly divulging confounding's sour fruit
With destructive seeds destroying soul-mind.
Silent mental tangles wither mind's root,
Covers perception with death's blackest suit
En route to misplaced memory once pined—
Portend change's grief, bedevils thought's route,
Decrying stolen thoughts forever moot
As lifelong experiences unwind.
Silent mental tangles wither mind's root,
Lifetime memories nevermore astute.
Yet mercy's love supplants lost thoughts in kind
While Providence balms dark confusion's brute.
Silent mental tangles wither mind's root,
Portend change's grief, bedevils thought's route,
Replaces bereavement with loving's mind—
While Providence balms dark confusion's brute.

Brandt Triadic Villanelle
Relationship III.3

III.2

I miss my mom, the talks we had,
Time we spent when discussions droll;
Yet ache remains—sad just a tad.
Dark chocolate shakes made us glad,
Were protein-packed for weight gain goal.
I miss my mom, the talks we had,
With kids and grands and me, granddad,
Grandma too, each played our role.
Remembering this makes me sad,
This last time they saw her glad
Yet time was short to living's dole.
I miss my mom, the talks we had,
The final calls before death's gad
When last appointment left a hole.
Yet ache remains—sad just a tad.
I miss my mom, the talks we had,
Remembering this makes me sad
Though gratitude does seize my soul,
Yet ache remains—sad just a tad.

Brandt Triadic Villanelle

III.2
My Mother's Legacy

A few months back I was visiting my mom. She'd had some health issues, and Cheryl and I stopped by often to help. I miss that.

Nutrition was a concern, so we brought dark-chocolate protein shakes. We'd share one as we talked. I miss that.

In September we returned with two of our sons, a daughter-in-law, and grandchildren—the last time my children saw their grandmother alive. After we left, I called her daily. I miss that too.

In October Mom passed away after a long, full life. I'm grateful for her years, her lessons, and her love—but gratitude doesn't soften the ache. I still miss my mom.

III.3

Deep binding sorrow possesses us,
A biting, consuming dark roast coffee.
Then each poem opens and deepens.
This journey of grief bears retelling,
Is ours to cherish and ours to value;
Deep binding sorrow possesses us.
Monsoon rain stings us like sharp hail,
Plants wail overwhelmed by water.
Then each poem opens and deepens.
We've stopped being obsessed with deception,
While exhausted sleepers deeply slumber,
Deep binding sorrow possesses us.
The poem's dancing jester grows but brash,
As the crumbling alpine pass grows steep,
Then each poem opens and deepens.
The Redeemer's life redeemed the elect,
The faithful harvest what kindness plants;
Deep binding sorrow possesses us,
Then each poem opens and deepens.

III.3
Grieving Cord's Gold

The heavy cords of grief now take their hold,
A bitter brew consumed both dark and deep.
Yet every verse begins its turn to gold.
The story borne from sorrow often told,
Is ours to treasure and is ours to keep;
The heavy cords of grief now take their hold.
Torrential rain does bite us sharp and cold,
The roots that drown begin to cry and weep,
Yet every verse begins its turn to gold.
No longer by a stupid lie controlled,
While tired somnambulants do soundly sleep,
The heavy cords of grief now take their hold.
The rhythm rhyming joker grows quite bold,
While the broken mountain path rises steep,
Yet every verse begins its turn to gold.
The Savior's hand has bought the chosen fold,
What mercy sows, the faithful soul shall reap;
The heavy cords of grief now take their hold,
Yet every verse begins its turn to gold.

Redemptions Refrain IV.7 with revisions to line 4 and 14.

III.4

You gave your all to fill my soul
And shepherded me beside,
The clinging and uncertain lad
From ages past bygone.
Now Providence took you from my life
To heaven up above,
The lad that thrived, the clay you formed—
Complete, a standalone.

III.4
My Mother's Gift

You poured your life full into mine
And mothered me along,
The insecure, dependent boy
From years ago is gone.
So though God moved you off this earth
To your eternal home,
The boy you grew, the man you made—
Able to stand alone.

Deliverance Acknowledgments and *Redemptions Refrain* IV.6

III.5

Tender hands still mold with grace
Feeding father at gentle pace,
All these things are praise's base.
Time well spent though vacant face,
Silent times are commonplace,
Tender hands still mold with grace.
Full time care in sterile place
Tending pain, knowledge effaced.
Small kindnesses ne'er done in haste,
Daughter's love tenderly placed—
All combined and interlaced.
Tender hands still mold with grace,
Joyful time with simple tastes—
Spiced applesauce then tastebuds graced—
All these things are praise's base.
Tender hands still mold with grace,
Small kindnesses ne'er done in haste,
Near the goal of his life's race,
All these things are praise's base.

Brandt Triadic Villanelle

III.5
Father's Applesauce

Cheryl and I have spent the last six mealtimes with her nearly ninety-three-year-old father. He lives in a nursing home, needs full-time care, suffers chronic pain, and is unable to articulate his needs. Our time together has held little recognition of our presence—no clear sign of pleasure—until tonight.

Tonight's meal included hot spiced applesauce. With his first bite, he shook and smiled at the taste. It was a joy for all of us.

I hope as I move forward in life, I remember what this brief time has taught me: watching his daughter care for him—gently caressing his shoulders and feeding him—reminds me that simple acts are often the ones most worthy of praise.

Hold by Grace

Coda
Obsession's Freedom

Why does my mind obsess over thee?
Obsession snares freedom, yet I'm free.
Although obsessed, I am still not bound;
Mind energized, freedom truly found.

Why, then, daily does obsession bind,
Creating yearnings, compelling mind?
Is it bondage to new thoughts in me,
Or awareness of my freedom's glee?

Yes, my mind to freedom does obsess,
Every day seized my soul to possess,
Desire waxed full, enveloped by joy;
This sweet grace does give life to enjoy.

Redemptions VI.5

Turn

by

Grace

Envoi
Dead End's Illusion

Gentle slope ahead.
Wall hinders progress forward—
Illusion. Turn right.

Redemptions Refrain III.8

Subsequent volumes in *Redemptions Rhythms: Interpretive Companion* extend this framework into other lived experiences, carrying forward the same pairing of a structured Message and its Interpretive Companion.

Books in this Series

Foundation Triad

Redemptions: Six Cycles from Sin to Stubborn Joy

Deliverance: Five Cycles from Doom—Up from the Gloom

Redemptions Refrain: Five Cycles from Play to Steady Grace

Pastoral Triad

The Relationship Companion: Providence, the Marriage Bond, and Cognitive Decline

The Caregiver Companion: Love's Burden and Holding On through His Mercy

Up Next—

The Sufferer Companion: The Breaking, the Weight, and the Turning

www.ingramcontent.com/pod-product-compliance
Lightning Source LLC
LaVergne TN
LVHW050749061126
851857LV00013B/1067
* 9 7 9 8 3 8 5 2 9 2 0 9 7 *